The Widow Next Door

Ebrima Dembajang

Ukiyoto Publishing

All global publishing rights are held by

Ukiyoto Publishing

Published in 2024

Content Copyright © Ebrima Dembajang

ISBN 9789364946261

All rights reserved.

No part of this publication may be reproduced, transmitted, or stored in a retrieval system, in any form by any means, electronic, mechanical, photocopying, recording or otherwise, without the prior permission of the publisher.

The moral rights of the author have been asserted.

This book is sold subject to the condition that it shall not by way of trade or otherwise, be lent, resold, hired out or otherwise circulated, without the publisher's prior consent, in any form of binding or cover other than that in which it is published.

www.ukiyoto.com

DEDICATION

This book is wholeheartedly dedicated to my beloved Village, Jarra Jiffen, Minister of Interior, Hon. Abdoulie Sanyang. The Inspector General of Gambia Police Force, Seedy Touray; Chief of Defense Staff, Mamar O Cham, My beloved mother, Nato Fadera, the inspiring Jalika Cham and finally my father, Bakary Dembajang.

ACKNOWLEDGMENT

I want to acknowledge the great contribution of my former teacher, Mr. Momodou Nabaan, best friend Mariama Ceesay, my loyal comrade Faback Gibba, and to all the remarkable individuals who has contributed to my personal development.

Contents

Chapter One - The Tragic Loss	1
Chapter Two - The Abandoned And Alonely Amina	5
Chapter Three - The Descent Into Desperation	9
Chapter Four - Bakary's Friend	12
Chapter Five - The Hidden Secrets	16
Chapter Six - A New Beginning	18
Chapter Seven - The Envious Family	21
Chapter Eight - Bakary's Foundation	24
Chapter Nine - Amina Met Lamin	27
Chapter Ten - The Price of Greed	30
Chapter Evelen - Tears Of Betrayal And Heartbreak	32
Chapter Twelve - Rising From The Ashes, Once Again	34
Chapter Thirteen - A Community Celebration	37
About the Author	*41*

Chapter One - The Tragic Loss

In a small village located in the heart of Lower River Region called Jiffen, there lived a humble and beautiful widow named Amina. She and her husband, Bakary, had always dreamed of a better life for themselves and their future children. The village they called home was overrun by poverty and surrounded by limited opportunities, leaving them with little hope for a brighter future.

One day, Bakary came across stories of people who had successfully migrated to Spain in search of better opportunities. Most of these stories are centered on people who took diverse irregular paths to reach Europe and eventually changed the socio-economic conditions of themselves, their families and some friends. The promise of a stable income and a chance to provide for their family ignited a spark of hope within him. Crossing checking and taking better pictures of those "Semesters " couldn't get off Bakary. After much contemplation, thoughts and consideration with the few individuals that slightly made changes in Jiffen and surrounding villages, Bakary made the difficult decision to embark on the dangerous and unsafe journey to Spain, leaving behind his beloved wife, Amina.

Leaving and creating space for Amina which was never a dreamt thought ever in their matrimonial house. The joy of a husband and wife was so mutual and undistracted and has shown and gain admiration in the Village of Jiffen. With a heavy heart, Amina bid farewell to Bakary, praying for his safety and success. She knew the risks involved in

irregular migration, commonly known as the " Backway, " but she has trusted Bakary's determination and believed that his sacrifice would be worthwhile. With the believe of life changing and dream building story, Amina uses her joy to surpassed the painful reality of staying alone while your partner paddles with the uncertain route of life.

Days turned into weeks, and weeks into months, yet there was no word from Bakary. Amina anxiously awaited news of his arrival in Spain, hoping for a sign that he had made it safely. But as time passed, her hope began to fade, replaced by a great sense of dread. Amina could no longer enjoy the foods she eats. She lost weight and her face depicts a sign of unhappiness despite her charming look. Her facial look speaks more words than her mouth.

The first news of tragic accidents and hazardous journeys reached the village at the hours of noon, casting a dark shadow over Amina's heart. She couldn't help but fear the worst, imagining the dangers Bakary might have faced in his quest for a better life. The uncertainty weighed heavily on her, and she found solace only in her prayers and the support of her community.

Months turned into a year, and Amina's worst fears were confirmed. Word reached the village that Bakary had answered the call of his ancestors during his journey to Spain. The unwanted news shattered Amina's world, leaving her devastated and alone. The dreams they had shared were now nothing more than shattered fragments of what could have been.

The grief that engulfed Amina was unlike anything she had ever experienced. The pain of losing her husband was unbearable, and the realization that she would never see him again ripped at her soul. The village mourned alongside her, offering their condolences

and support, but their sympathy could never fill the emptiness in her heart.

Amina's days became a blur of sorrow and longing. Every corner of their modest home held memories of Bakary, reminding her of the love they had shared and the dreams they had nurtured. She clung to those memories, finding solace in the moments they had cherished together.

As the months passed, Bakary's grief began to transform into a quiet determination. She felt the need to be strong and navigate through the existing hurdles with a strong faith and the zeal to reshape her own life. She very well knew she had to carry on, not just for herself but for Bakary's memory. She became more determined to honor her sacrifice and find a way to provide for herself, despite the challenges that lay ahead.

Little did Amina know that her journey was just beginning. The path before her was filled with hardship, but deep within her, a flicker of resilience burned. She would face the struggles that awaited her, drawing strength from the love she had shared with Bakary and the dreams they had once held so dear.

Chapter Two - The Abandoned And Alonely Amina

With Bakary gone, Amina's world smashed into a million pieces. The loss of her beloved husband was devastating enough, but what followed was a heart-wrenching betrayal by Bakary's own family. Blinded by their grief and burdened cultural expectations, they cast Amina aside, believing that without a child, she was no longer of any value. It was as if her worth had been reduced to her ability to bear offspring. The measure used to measure her strength and power was nothing but a child and forgetting her sacrifices she put across the line.

The pain of abandonment cut deep, leaving Amina feeling utterly alone and vulnerable. She had always believed that family was supposed to be a source of love and support, especially during times of hardship. But now, she found herself tussling with the harsh reality that her in-laws had turned their backs on her, leaving her to navigate the unsafe path of life on her own. Amina started sensing betrayal from the people who ought to be her support system.

The days that followed were a constant struggle for survival. Amina, once familiarized with a comfortable life, was now propelled into a world where she had to fight for every atom of food on the table. She took on odd jobs, working tirelessly to make ends meet, but the wages were small, barely enough to sustain her basic needs. The once vibrant and lively woman became a mere shell of her former self, her spirit drained by

the weight of her circumstances.

While Bakary's mother and Father are sitting, Amina is left sitting under her lonely sadden container of sorrow. She was made to feel like an inland and the partial presence of her in-laws couldn't make changes for her situation. Loneliness continues to become Amina's constant companion. The absence of Bakary's presence was a void that seemed impossible to fill. She yearned for his comforting embrace, his reassuring words, and his unwavering support. All she had were memories, memories that brought both joy and sorrow, reminding her of a love that was unexpectedly stolen from her.

As the days turned into weeks, Amina's resilience began to waver. The burden of her situation weighed heavily on her shoulders, threatening to crush her spirit. She wondered how she would ever find the strength to carry on, to face the world that had turned its back on her. But deep within her, an indication of determination remained a glimmer of hope that refused to be demolished.

Amina knew that she had to rise above her circumstances. She had to prove to herself and to the world that she was more than just a dumped wife. With every slight of strength she could muster, she pushed forward, refusing to let despair define her. She sought solace in the smallest victories, finding joy in the simplest of pleasures.

Slowly but surely, Amina battle to rebuild her life. She discovered a newfound independence and resilience within herself, realizing that she was capable of so much more than she had ever imagined. She wonder when will she find solace in the support of kind-hearted strangers hence her matrimonial home is a hell for existence when will she find solace in the support of kind-hearted strangers hence her matrimonial home is a hell for existence. Offering a helping hand or a word of encouragement was her words of prayers. She remained faithful and avoids the blame game with the spirit that she must continue to make differences for herself despite the unfortunate circumstances.

In the midst of her struggle, Amina also found a renewed sense of purpose. She became determined to break free from the bonds of societal expectations and redefine her own worth. She vowed to build a life that was not defined by her marital status or her ability to bear children, but by her strength, resilience, and compassion even though it was impossible as the struggles championed the dreams. And so, Amina's path continued, filled with both triumphs and setbacks. But through it all, she remained steadfast in her determination, commitment and hard work to forge her own destiny. She may have been abandoned and left to fend for herself, but she refused to let that by any means define her. Amina was a survivor, and she would not be defeated.

Chapter Three - The Descent Into Desperation

As the weeks turned into months, Amina's daunting struggle for survival intensified, tumbling her deeper into the deep of desperation. The once vibrant, charming and determined woman now found herself facing the harsh realities of poverty and hunger, her spirit slowly being severely corrupted by the relentless challenges that life threw her way.

With each passing day, Amina's situation grew more severe. The odd jobs she had relied on to make ends meet became inadequate, leaving her with no choice but to resort to begging just to sustain herself. The humiliation and shame that accompanied this desperate act weighed heavily on her soul, but the gnawing hunger in her stomach pushed her to swallow her pride.

Amina's days became a never-ending cycle of searching for scraps, pleading for help, and enduring the arrogant glances of passersby. She felt invisible, as if she had become a mere shadow in a world that had forgotten her existence. once as if she had become a mere shadow in a world that had forgotten her existence. The once unrest streets now seemed cold and indifferent, a stark contrast to the warmth and compassion she had once believed in.

The hunger that ground at Amina's stomach was not just physical; it was a hunger for dignity, for a sense of purpose, for a glimmer of hope. She yearned for a life that was not defined by her circumstances, a life where she could stand tall and proud, free from the chains of poverty and despair that dropped on her innocent because of the dangerous irregular migration (Backway).

But as the days stretched on, Amina's spirit began to weaken. The weight of her circumstances bore down on her, threatening to crush her fragile resolve. She found herself in a troubling dilemma. She questioned whether she had the strength to continue fighting, whether there was any light at the end of this seemingly endless underpass.

Loneliness became an unwelcome companion, adding to the burden that Amina carried. The absence of companionship and support left her feeling isolated and disconnected from the world around her. She longed for someone to understand her struggles, but the dream of offering a helping hand or a word of encouragement was still unrealistic. In her darkest moments, it seemed as though she was truly alone with no sign of help.

As desperation consumed her, Amina's dreams and aspirations faded into the background. The once bright spark of hope that had fueled her determination now flickered weakly, threatening to be destroyed. She questioned whether she had the strength to keep going, whether her life would ever improve, or if she was destined to be trapped in this cycle of despair forever.

But even in the depths of her desperation, a small voice within Amina refused to be silenced. It reminded her of the resilience she had shown in the face of adversity, the strength she had discovered within herself. It whispered tales of others who had risen from the depths of despair and found their way to a better life. And in that whisper, a

glimmer of hope began to flicker once more.

Amina knew that she had to find the strength to keep going, to continue fighting for a better future. She refused to let her circumstances define her, to let desperation consume her. With every ounce of determination she could muster, she pushed forward, clinging to that flicker of hope, no matter how faint.

And so, Amina's descent into desperation became a turning point in her journey. Will it be a moment of reckoning, a catalyst for change? She knew that she had to find a way to rise above her circumstances, to reclaim her dignity and rebuild her life. The road ahead was uncertain and dangerous, but Amina was determined to forge ahead, to rewrite her story, and to prove that even in the darkest of times, there is always a glimmer of hope.

Chapter Four - Bakary's Friend

One fateful day, as Amina sat on a dusty street corner, her tattered clothes blending with the desolation around her, she caught the attention of a familiar face. It was Bakary's childhood friend, Yankuba, who had also migrated to Spain but returned home after facing hardships of his own. The sight of him awakened a mix of emotions within Amina - surprise, memories, and a glimmer of hope.

Yankuba, a kind-hearted soul, had always shared a strong bond with Bakary. Their friendship had weathered the storms of life, and even though circumstances had unfortunately pulled them apart, their connection remained intact. As he approached Amina, his eyes filled with both sorrow and empathy, it was as if a lifeline had been thrown to her in the midst of her despair. He took seconds to wonder whether he is dreaming.

At that moment, Amina felt a thrill of emotions flood through her. The familiarity of Yankuba's face brought back memories of happier times, reminding her of the love and support she had once known. It was a bittersweet reminder of the life she had lost but also a spark of hope that perhaps, just perhaps, there was a chance for rescue.

Yankuba's presence was a lifeline, a glimmer of hope in the darkness that had consumed Amina's world. He listened intently as she poured out her heart, sharing the depths of her struggles and the pain of her abandonment. His eyes filled with tears as he absorbed the magnitude of her suffering, and in that moment, Amina felt seen and heard.

Moved by Amina's plight, Yankuba couldn't believe but made a promise to himself and to her. He vowed to help her rise from the depths of despair, to offer her a chance at a better life. With unwavering determination, he set out to find resources, connections, and opportunities that could provide Amina with the support she desperately needed.

Days turned into weeks as Yankuba tirelessly searched for solutions. He reached out to local organizations, seeking assistance for Amina's plight. He connected with individuals who were willing to offer her employment, a safe place to stay, and a support system that could help her rebuild her life. Amina watched in awe as the pieces of her shattered world slowly began to come together.

The glimmer of hope that had ignited within Amina grew brighter and stronger with each passing moment. She started to believe that there is a promising future beyond her current circumstances, that she could reclaim her dignity and find happiness once again. The support and guidance provided by Yankuba reminded her that she was not alone, that there were people who cared and were willing to help her on her journey.

As Amina embraced the opportunities that came her way, she once more discovered a newfound strength within herself. The hardships she had endured had not broken her; instead, they had forged and molded her into a resilient and determined woman. Will she channel her pain into motivation, using it as fuel to rebuild her life and withstand the odds stacked against her?

With Yankuba's unwavering support and the newfound resources at her disposal, Amina started to piece her life back together. She found stable employment, allowing her to provide for her basic needs and regain a sense of independence. She surrounded herself with a network of compassionate individuals who uplifted and encouraged her, reminding her of her inherent worth.

The glimmer of hope that had once seemed so distant now burned brightly within Amina's heart. She began to dream again, envisioning a future filled with possibilities. The wounds of her past were far from healed, but she had embarked on a journey of healing and self-discovery, determined to rewrite her story and create a life that was truly her own.

As Amina's story spread, it became an inspiration to others facing similar struggles. Her resilience and determination served as a beacon of hope, reminding them that even in the darkest of times, there is always a glimmer of hope. Amina's journey was a testament to the power of human connection, the strength that can be found in the kindness of strangers, and the transformative power of hope.

And so, Amina's life continued to unfold, guided by the glimmer of hope that had

ignited within her. She knew that her journey was far from over, that there would be obstacles and setbacks along the way. But armed with resilience, determination, and the support of those who believed in her, she was ready to face whatever challenges lay ahead, knowing that she had the power to shape her own destiny.

Chapter Five - The Hidden Secrets

Shocked by Amina's story, Yankuba's curiosity drove him to further investigate the circumstances involving his late friend's wife, Amina. He couldn't shake the feeling that there was more to Bakary's disappearance in the sea than met the eye. With a determination to uncover the truth, he delved into the depths of the secret that surrounded Amina's husband.

Yankuba began by making discreet inquiries with Bakary's friends and other relatives that who knew about Bakary, hoping to gain insight into his sudden departure and the subsequent abandonment of Amina. It was during these conversations and fact findings that he encountered a shocking revelation that Bakary had left behind a significant amount of money, a vast compound, and a thriving business that had grown in his absence.

The discovery left Yankuba speechless, unable to comprehend how such a secret could have remained hidden from Amina and the rest of Bakary's family. It was a revelation that shattered the perception they had held of their departed loved one, and it raised countless questions about the motives behind his sudden death in the sea and the abandoning of Amina.

As Yankuba dug deeper, he uncovered the complexness of Bakary's hidden success. It appeared that, unbeknownst to his family, Bakary had achieved great wealth and prosperity before his untimely demise. He had built a thriving business empire, one that had flourished in the shadows, away from the prying eyes of his loved ones.

The revelation of Bakary's hidden secrets sent shockwaves through Amina's world. It was a bittersweet realization, as she grappled with conflicting emotions. On one hand, she felt a sense of betrayal, questioning why Bakary had kept his success hidden from her and his family. On the other hand, she couldn't help but feel a glimmer of hope for the possibilities that this newfound knowledge presented.

The discovery of Bakary's wealth and assets opened up a world of opportunities for Amina. It meant that she no longer had to rely solely on the kindness of others or struggle to make ends meet. It offered her a chance to reclaim her independence and rebuild a future and made the dreams of the gone husband a success.

Chapter Six - A New Beginning

As Amina stood in the midst of the bustling marketplace, a newfound sense of purpose filled her heart. The knowledge she had gained from the revelation of Bakary's friend and her encounter with the wise old woman during the times of her begging had ignited a flame within her, urging her to take control of her own destiny. With each step she took, she felt her confidence grow, fueled by the support and encouragement of Yankuba, her steadfast companion.

Together, Amina and Yankuba embarked on a journey to reclaim her rightful place in the community. They faced numerous challenges along the way, as societal

expectations and prejudices weighed heavily against them. But Amina's determination and Yankuba ' s unwavering belief in her abilities kept them pushing forward, undeterred by the obstacles that lay in their path.

Word of Amina ' s transformation began to spread like wildfire through the town. People who had once dismissed her as a helpless widow now witnessed her resilience and strength. They saw her withstand the limitations imposed upon her by society, breaking free from the shackles of traditional gender roles. Amina became a symbol of hope, inspiring others to overcome their own hardships and strive for a better future.

The once marginalized members of the community found solace in Amina's story. They saw a reflection of their own struggles and were inspired to stand up against the injustices that haunted their lives. Amina's journey became a catalyst for change, as people began to question the rigid norms that had held them back for so long.

But Amina's transformation was not without its share of resistance. There were those who feared the disruption of the status quo, threatened by the empowerment she represented. They tried to undermine her efforts, spreading rumors and casting doubt on her intentions. Yet, Amina remained steadfast, refusing to let their negativity moisten her spirit. She proved to be that woman who is carefully careless to things that matters less.

In the face of adversity, Amina found allies in unexpected places. People who had once turned a blind eye to her struggles now rallied behind her, offering their support and lending their voices to the cause. The community began to unite, forming a powerful network of change-makers determined to challenge the oppressive norms that had held them back for far too long.

As Amina's influence grew, so did her impact on the lives of those around her. She established support networks for other widows, providing them with the tools and resources they needed to rebuild their lives. She fought for equal rights and opportunities for women, advocating for their inclusion in decision-making processes and breaking down the barriers that had confined them to the sidelines. This will never go down well with evil doers and their associates.

Amina knew that her journey was far from over, but with each passing day, she grew stronger and more resilient. The seeds of change she had planted began to take root, spreading hope and empowerment throughout the community. Her story became a living testament to the power of determination and the ability to rise above adversity.

What is next? What are the challenges that lie ahead for Amina and the community she has inspired? As the winds of change continue to blow, new conflicts and obstacles continue to arise, testing the strength of their convictions. But with Amina leading the way, armed with her newfound knowledge and unwavering determination, she has no doubt that they will overcome whatever comes their way.

Chapter Seven - The Envious Family

The news of Amina's remarkable transformation traveled swiftly through the town, capturing the attention of Bakary's family. Consumed by envy and regret, they could not help but feel a discomfort of jealousy at Amina's newfound wealth and success. Suddenly, their indifference towards her turned into a desperate attempt to reconcile, driven solely by their desire to benefit from her newfound fortune.

The envious family, realizing the error of their ways, saw an opportunity to mend the broken bonds with Amina. They approached her with seemingly genuine gestures,

hoping to gain access to her wealth and prosperity. But Amina, now wise to their true intentions, refused to be swayed by their deceitful acts.

Having endured years of mistreatment and neglect at the hands of Bakary's family, Amina had learned to recognize their true colors. She had experienced firsthand their indifference and lack of support during her darkest moments. Amina knew that their sudden interest in her was fueled by envy, not genuine care or remorse.

With a newfound sense of self-worth and resilience, Amina stood her ground. She refused to let Bakary's family exploit her success for their own gain. Her refusal to reconcile with them was not an act of revenge, but rather an act of self-preservation. Amina had worked tirelessly to rebuild her life, and she was determined to protect her newfound happiness from those who had once disregarded her.

As news of Amina's rejection spread, the envious family grew increasingly resentful. Fueled by bitterness, they resorted to spreading rumors and gossip, hoping to tarnish her reputation and bring her down. However, Amina 's unwavering strength and the support of her newfound community shielded her from their malicious attempts.

The village been in the midst of the whole narration and an eyewitness to the struggles of Amina, knew very well that hatred was at its highest level of stance. The family of Bakary turned into plan two in finding happiness to their jealousy just to see Amina down. Bakary's mum and dad had to leave for Jarra Barrow Kunda to visit a spiritual man for the solution to the problem they caused on their selves.

Lightness never hides in the presence of darkness. Amina has given so much help and holds a clean heart that is pure and cannot be down by darkness. The man knows that the zeal and determination embedded in the wife of their late son can never be destroyed easily, but ego cannot allow him to forgo his unwarranted and unnoticed evil intentions. The feedback obtained from the host marabout is not the most welcoming feedback for Bakary's mum and dad after traveling for kilometers to find an alternative recipe for Amina's downfall.

This was not the best for them and to explore for more means was going to be the next moves. In the heart where worthiness has no value, the products and fruits have no or less impact. Amina continue to believe that her resilience will never be shaken nor crippled.

Chapter Eight - Bakary's Foundation

Inspired by her own journey of transformation, Amina made the conscious decision to use her newfound wealth and power to uplift those in need. Instead of accumulating her resources for personal gain, she established a foundation dedicated to providing education, healthcare, and support to the most vulnerable members of the community. Amina's generosity and compassion soon became legendary, earning her the respect and admiration of all.

Amina believes that its humanity before any other thing and to render service is nothing but human. The foundation was meant to leverage and liberate those in the hardship of society. She wants to use the association as an instrumental tool to help those that have been sidelined by cultural expectations and societal norms and values within the community.

Through her foundation, Amina sought to address the systemic inequalities and barriers that had held back individuals in her community. She recognized that education is indeed the key to unlocking opportunities and breaking the cycle of poverty that remains to be the overall enemy in many societies. With this in mind, she established scholarship programs, ensuring that children from disadvantaged backgrounds had access to quality education.

Amina 's foundation also focused on providing healthcare services to those who had previously been neglected or unable to afford proper medical care. She built a clinic in the community and partnered with healthcare professionals to offer free and subsidized treatments to those in need. Amina believed that good health was not a privilege reserved for the wealthy, but a basic human right that should be accessible to all.

But Amina 's impact extended beyond education and healthcare. She recognized the importance of providing emotional and psychological support to those who had experienced trauma or loss. Amina established counseling and support programs, offering a safe space for individuals to heal and rebuild their lives. Through these initiatives, she aimed to empower others to overcome their hardships and embrace their own potential.

As news of Amina's foundation spread, the community rallied behind her cause once more time. People from all walks of life came forward to contribute their time, skills, and resources to support her mission. The unity and collective effort that emerged were a testament to the power of Amina's vision and the impact she had on those around her.

Bakary's foundation became a beacon of hope, not just in her own community but also in neighboring towns and villages. Her story inspired others to take action and make a difference in their own communities.

Schools and organizations often call Amina to their programs to give lectures or serve as guest speaker. The ripple effect of her generosity and compassion began to extend far beyond what she had initially imagined.

Bakary's foundation continues to prove itself to be a nonprofit making adventure, and it thrives with a sheer consistency on its selfless services to the community thanks to the commitment, determination, patience and hard work of Amina. The foundation's name became a familiar name to news enthusiasts and social media users. It serves as a reference for many people including musicians development analysts.

Chapter Nine - Amina Met Lamin

Amidst Amina's tireless efforts to uplift her community through her foundation, fate had a gigantic surprise in store for her. In the midst of her philanthropic endeavors, she crossed paths with Lamin, a kind-hearted widower who had also experienced the

profound pain of loss. Lamin has gone through a lot of struggles that has made him to have or build less hope. He thinks it will never be luck for him to have a partner as his late wife.

Their shared experiences and mutual understanding formed the foundation for a deep and meaningful connection, bringing love and companionship back into Amina's life.

Lamin, like Amina, had gone through his own journey of healing and self-discovery after the loss of his spouse. Their paths converged at a community event organized by Bakary's foundation, where they found themselves drawn to each other's warmth and compassion. As they spent more time together, their connection deepened, and they discovered a shared sense of purpose and a desire to make a lasting impact on the world around them.

Their relationship flourished amidst the backdrop of their collective efforts to empower others. Amina and Lamin became pillars of support for one another, understanding the unique challenges they had faced as a widow and widower respectively and finding solace in each other's presence. They provided a safe space for healing, allowing their love to grow and flourish.

Their love story became an inspiration to the community, demonstrating that even amidst hardship, there is always room for love and companionship. Amina and Lamin's relationship reminded others that it is never too late to find happiness and that love can be rediscovered even after experiencing profound loss. The duo continues to be referenced by so many people in their community.

As Amina and Lamin 's love story unfolded, their shared vision for a better future

became even more powerful. They combined their resources and talents, joining forces to expand the reach of Bakary's foundation and make an even greater impact on the lives of those in need. Together, they spearheaded new initiatives, addressing pressing issues such as gender inequality, access to clean water, and environmental sustainability.

The community witnessed firsthand the power of love and unity as Amina and Lamin worked side by side, inspiring others to join their cause. Their relationship became a symbol of hope and resilience, showing that love can be a driving force for positive change. People began to recognize that by coming together, they could overcome any obstacle and create a brighter future for all.

Chapter Ten - The Price of Greed

As Amina's life continued to flourish, there were individuals within the village who couldn ' t bear to witness her well deserved success despite the numerous help she continues to render humanity. Envy and greed bled into their hearts, fueling a desire to exploit Amina's newfound wealth for their own gain. Unbeknownst to her, they plotted in the shadows, developing a plan to deceive her and manipulate her into denying her fortune.

These individuals saw Amina's generosity and compassion as an opportunity to fulfill their own selfish desires. They believed that by deceiving her, they could gain access to her wealth and live a life of luxury at her expense. Their greed blinded them to the impact their actions would have on Amina and the community she had worked so hard to uplift.

The plot to exploit Amina 's wealth unfolded slowly, with the individuals carefully crafting a web of lies and deceit. They approached her with false stories of hardship and need, pretending to be in desperate situations that only her wealth could alleviate. Their manipulative tactics were designed to prey on Amina ' s kind heart and willingness to help others.

Little did they know, Amina's journey had taught her valuable lessons about discernment and resilience. While her heart remained open to those in need, she had developed a keen intuition that allowed her to see through the masks of deception. Amina had become wise to the ways of the world and could sense when someone's intentions were not genuine.

As the individuals carried out their plan, Amina's intuition began to raise red flags. She noticed inconsistencies in their stories and detected a hint of greed in their eyes. Rather than confront them directly, Amina decided to gather evidence and expose their deceitful intentions to protect herself and the community from their harmful actions.

In her quest to expose and prevent the community from the evil doers, she has to pay

the price of the evilness of human. With her hard work to prevent and block the greed of enemies, she wasn't able to detect all to prevent.

With the help of trusted allies within the village, Amina uncovered some truth behind the plot to exploit her wealth. She invited some women for lunch at her house and allowed them to blow the doings and evils of their friends, not knowing that those narrators were part of the planners. She discovered the identities of those involved and the extent of their greed-driven scheme. Armed with this knowledge, Amina devised a counterplan to turn the tables on her would-be exploiters.

Chapter Evelen - Tears Of Betrayal And Heartbreak

Trusting the wrong people proved to be Amina's downfall. Despite her intuition and resilience, she felt to be a victim to a cunning scheme orchestrated by those she had once considered friends and those enemies she wasn't able to detect during her quest to protect and block herself from the greed of the evil doers. They skillfully manipulated

her emotions, deceived her with false promises, and ultimately fooled her out of a significant portion of her hard-earned wealth. Amina 's heart shattered into a million pieces as she realized the depths of human betrayal.

The individuals who had plotted to exploit Amina's wealth had carefully cultivated a deception of friendship and trust. They had ingratiated themselves into her life, gaining her confidence and making her believe that they were genuine allies. Amina, driven by her desire to help others, had unknowingly opened herself up to their deceitful tactics.

To her more and shocking disappointment, Yankuba's younger sister, whom she considered her best friend after crossing paths with Yankuba, is at the zenith of the betrayal. This was her biggest setback and surprise because she never knew it was in the pipeline. She always knew her to be a very caring, compassionate and trust looking woman in the entire village of Jarra Jiffen.

It was a devastating blow when Amina discovered the truth. The realization that those she had trusted had betrayed her trust and taken advantage of her generosity left her feeling not only deceived but also deeply hurt. The weight of the betrayal was almost unbearable, threatening to crush her spirit and undo all the progress she had made in rebuilding her life.

In the aftermath of the betrayal, Amina found herself questioning her own judgment and the true nature of human beings. She grappled with feelings of anger, sadness, and profound disappointment. The wounds inflicted by the betrayal ran deep, leaving scars that would take time to heal.

However, Amina's strength and resilience were not easily extinguished. She refused to let the betrayal define her or dictate the course of her life. Instead, she channeled her pain into a renewed determination to rebuild and rise above the heartbreak. Amina drew strength from the support of her true allies and the unwavering belief in her own worth.

Amina knew it was because of her generosity and success that she was pinpoint as the prime target for those consumed by envy and greed. And despite her intuition and wisdom, she fell victim to their deceitful plot. The betrayal she experienced shattered her trust and left her questioning the motives of others.

Chapter Twelve - Rising From The Ashes, Once Again

Devastated by the profound betrayal she had endured, Amina found herself at rock bottom once more. The weight of the falsehood and the loss of her hard-earned wealth threatened to consume her spirit. But within the depths of her despair, a flicker of resilience emerged. Determined to reclaim her life and overcome the pain, she summoned the strength to rebuild what had been taken from her. Amina vowed to rise

from the ashes, stronger and wiser than ever before.

The journey of rebuilding was not an easy one. Amina had to confront her deepest fears and insecurities, facing the harsh reality of the betrayal she had experienced. She allowed herself to grieve the loss, acknowledging the pain and disappointment that had engulfed her heart. Through tears and moments of privacy, she began to heal, slowly stitching together the shattered pieces of her spirit.

Amina sought solace in the support of her true allies, those who had stood by her side through thick and thin. Their unwavering belief in her and their encouragement became the foundation upon which she could rebuild her life. With their guidance and love, she started to regain her confidence and trust in others, albeit cautiously.

As she embarked on the journey of rising from the ashes, Amina discovered a newfound strength within herself. The resilience that had carried her through previous hardships resurfaced, reminding her of the indomitable spirit she possessed. She refused to let the betrayal define her or hold her back from pursuing her dreams.

With each passing day, Amina took small steps towards reclaiming her life. She reevaluated her goals and aspirations, recalibrating her path to align with her newfound wisdom. Amina recognized that the true measure of her success was not solely defined by material wealth but by the impact she could make on the lives of others.

As she rebuilt her life, Amina also focused on fortifying her inner strength. She engaged in self-reflection, delving into her own vulnerabilities and fears, and emerged

with a renewed sense of self-awareness and self-love. Amina learned to trust her instincts once again, embracing the lessons learned from the betrayal as valuable tools for navigating future challenges.

We witnessed the devastating impact of the deceitful plot that had targeted Amina's wealth. The betrayal she experienced left her shattered and questioning the true nature of humanity. However, within the depths of her despair, she found the strength to rise again.

Chapter Thirteen - A Community Celebration

News of Amina's devastating plight spread like wildfire, reaching the ears of the wider community. The revelation of the numerous betrayal she had endured sparked a wave of outrage and compassion among those who had once benefited from her generosity. The villagers, deeply moved by her selflessness and the impact she had made on their lives, rallied together to support her in her time of need. They offered their assistance,

both in rebuilding her financial security and in restoring her faith in humanity.

The collective response from the community was overwhelming. People from all walks of life came forward, eager to lend a helping hand to Amina. They recognized that her unwavering dedication to uplifting others had been taken advantage of, and they were determined to right the wrongs that had been done to her.

Financial contributions poured in from individuals who had been touched by Amina's kindness. The community organized fundraisers, charity events, and donation drives to help rebuild her financial security. Every contribution, no matter how small, was a testament to the impact she had made on their lives. It was a powerful reminder of the interconnectedness of the community and the importance of standing together in times of adversity.

But it wasn't just financial support that Amina received. The villagers also offered their emotional support, eager to restore her faith in humanity. They surrounded her with love and kindness, reminding her that the actions of a few should not overshadow the goodness that existed within their community. Through their words and actions, they helped Amina heal the wounds of betrayal and regain her trust in others.

The unity and compassion displayed by the community had a profound impact on Amina. It reaffirmed her belief in the inherent goodness of people and restored her hope for a better future. She realized that the actions of a few should not define the entire community and that there were still countless individuals who shared her values of kindness and empathy.

As Amina's financial security began to stabilize and her faith in humanity was restored, she felt a deep sense of gratitude towards the community that had rallied around her. She knew that she would not have been able to rebuild her life without their unwavering support. Inspired by their collective efforts, Amina vowed to continue her mission of empowering others, knowing that together they could create a brighter and more compassionate world.

With the unwavering support of her community, Amina managed to rebuild her life once again. The collective efforts of the villagers, their financial contributions, and their emotional support played a crucial role in helping her regain her footing. The community stood as a testament to the power of unity and compassion, proving that when people come together, they can overcome even the most challenging of circumstances.

Through the process of rebuilding, Amina learned to trust again, albeit cautiously. The betrayal she had experienced had left deep scars, but she refused to let it define her. She recognized that not everyone was driven by greed and deceit, and she opened her heart to those who had shown her genuine kindness and support. Amina's journey of healing and resilience became an inspiration to all who knew her story.

Her ability to rise above adversity and rebuild her life became a beacon of hope for others facing their own challenges. Amina's legacy was not solely defined by her wealth, but by the hope she instilled in others. Her story served as a reminder that even in the darkest of times, there is always a glimmer of light to guide us forward.

As Amina continued her journey, she used her experiences and the lessons learned to

help those in need. Her generosity extended beyond material wealth; she shared her wisdom, her strength, and her unwavering belief in the power of compassion. Amina became a mentor and a source of inspiration for individuals who had lost their way, reminding them that they too could overcome their struggles and find hope in the face of adversity.

The impact of Amina's legacy rippled throughout the community, inspiring others to embrace kindness, empathy, and resilience. The villagers, touched by her story and the way she had risen from the ashes, carried forward her message of hope, spreading it to every corner of their lives. Amina's legacy became a catalyst for positive change, igniting a wave of compassion and unity that transformed the community for generations to come.

About the Author

Ebrima Dembajang

Ebrima Dembajang is a highly motivated and dedicated individual currently in his fourth year of pursuing a major in Development Studies at the esteemed University of The Gambia. His educational journey began at Scanaid Lower Basic School, where he laid the foundation for his future academic success. He continued his education at Scanaid Upper and Senior Secondary School, where he consistently demonstrated a commitment to excellence in all areas of his studies.

In addition to his academic pursuits, Ebrima is an active youth leader, utilizing his skills and knowledge to inspire and empower fellow young individuals. He firmly believes in the power of youth and their ability to bring about positive change in their communities. Ebrima is also a blogger, using his platform to raise awareness and engage with a wider audience on topics related to social issues, and current affairs.

With a strong academic background, leadership experience, and a passion for making a difference, Ebrima Dembajang is a dynamic individual poised to contribute significantly to the youthful population and bring about positive change in society.

www.ingramcontent.com/pod-product-compliance
Lightning Source LLC
LaVergne TN
LVHW041557070526
838199LV00046B/2015